Sizes

Heavy and Light

Diane Nieker

www.raintreepublishers.co.uk
Visit our website to find out more information about **Raintree** books.

To order:
 Phone 44 (0) 1865 888112
 Send a fax to 44 (0) 1865 314091
 Visit the Raintree Bookshop at **www.raintreepublishers.co.uk** to browse our catalogue and order online.

First published in Great Britain by Raintree, Halley Court, Jordan Hill, Oxford OX2 8EJ, part of Harcourt Education.
Raintree is a registered trademark of Harcourt Education Ltd.

Editorial: Sarah Shannon and Louise Galpine
Design: Jo Hinton-Malivoire
Picture Research: Natalie Gray and Ginny Stroud-Lewis
Production: Chloe Bloom
Originated by Dot Gradations UK
Printed and bound in China by South China Printing Company

ISBN 1844 43789 2
10 09 08 07 06
10 9 8 7 6 5 4 3 2 1

British Library Cataloguing in Publication Data
Nieker, Diane
Heavy and Light – (Sizes)
530.8'1

A full catalogue record for this book is available from the British Library.

Acknowledgements
Alamy Images/Transtock Inc. p. **13**; Corbis p. **19**; Digital Vision p. **14** (r); Getty Images/PhotoDisc pp. **12** (t), **14** (l), **15** (r); Harcourt Education/Tudor Photography pp. **4**, **5**, **6**, **7**, **8**, **9**, **10**, **11**, **17**, **18**, **21**; Science Photo Library p. **20** (Martyn F. Chillmaid); Transtock Inc./Alamy p. **12** (b).

Cover photograph reproduced with permission of Gareth Boden.

Every effort has been made to contact copyright holders of any material reproduced in this book. Any omissions will be rectified in subsequent printings if notice is given to the publishers.

The paper used to print this book comes from sustainable resources.

Some words are shown in bold, **like this**. They are explained in the glossary on page 23.

Contents

When is something light?

Something is **light** when it is easy to pick up and carry.

A **feather** is so light that you can hardly feel it on your hand.

Can one thing be lighter than another?

It is difficult for the girl to lift the scooter.

But it is easy for her to lift the toy bear.

The bear is lighter than the scooter.

Which is lightest?

Lightest means lighter than the others.

The box of crayons is lighter than the book.

The pencil is lighter than the box of crayons.

Which is lightest?

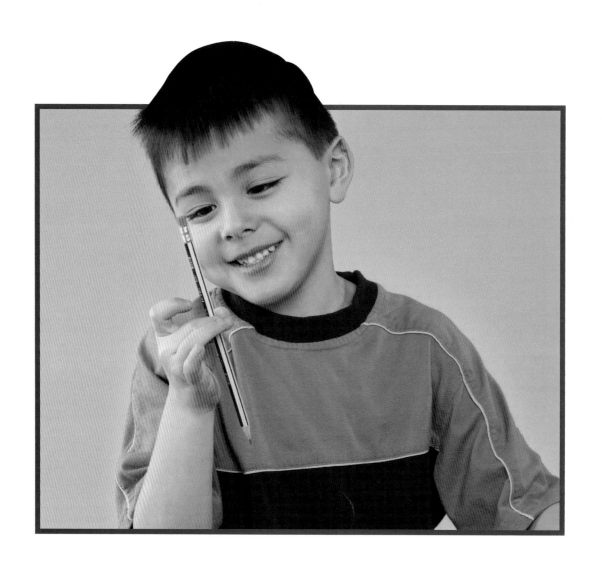

Did you say the pencil was lightest?

You were right!

What does heavy mean?

Something **heavy** is harder to lift than something **light**.

Which is heavier?

Which do you think is heavier, the bicycle or the car?

A car can carry a bicycle.

A bicycle cannot carry a car.

The car is heavier than the bicycle.

Which is heaviest?

Did you know that one car can be heavier than four zebras?

And one **elephant** can be as **heavy** as four cars.

Which is the heaviest, a zebra, an elephant, or a car?

If you said the elephant is heaviest, you were right!

Is something bigger always heavier?

Sometimes small things can be heavier than big things.

This grapefruit is heavier than the balloon.

How heavy is it?

When you pick something up, you know if it is **heavy**.

But you cannot tell how heavy it is.

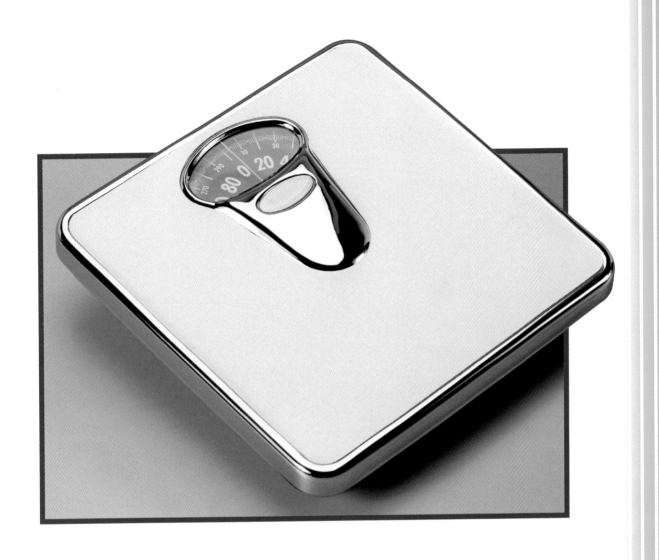

Scales help you measure how heavy things are.

What is weight?

When we talk about **heavy** and **light**, we are talking about weight.

Heavier things weigh more than lighter things.

This girl is finding her weight.

Do you know how much you weigh?

Quiz: True or False?

1. Weight means how **heavy** something is.

2. Things that are **light** do not weigh as much as things that are heavy.

3. A book is heavier than a **feather**.

4. Scales can tell you how much something weighs.

Glossary

 **elephant** large animal that has a trunk

 **feather** part of a bird. The outside of a bird is covered in feathers.

 **heavy** something that weighs a lot. A car is very heavy.

 **light** something that does not weigh very much. A toy bear is light.

Index

Answers to quiz on page 22

1. True

2. True

3. True

4. True

Note to parents and teachers

Reading non-fiction texts for information is an important part of a child's literacy development. Readers can be encouraged to ask simple questions and then use the text to find the answers. Most chapters in this book begin with a question. Read the questions together. Look at the pictures. Talk about what the answer might be. Then read the text to find out if your predictions were correct. To develop readers' enquiry skills, encourage them to think of other questions they might ask about the topic. Discuss where you could find the answers. Assist children in using the contents page, picture glossary, and index to practise research skills and new vocabulary.